The possibilities are endless when you use colorful paper scraps to craft creative Christmas gifts and décor. A nostalgic vintage look is easy with a joyful blend of old and new supplies.

# Holiday *Papercrafting*

LEISURE ARTS, INC. • Maumelle, Arkansas

# Framed Pen & Ink Santa

## SHOPPING LIST

- 12" square picture frame with glass
- India ink and dip pen
- toothpick
- 12" square cardstock for background
- 5" high numbers 2 and 5
- acrylic paints (dark brown and red) and paintbrush
- fine-grit sandpaper
- spray adhesive
- craft glue

1. Trace the pattern (page 16) onto the glass with the India ink and pen. Set aside to dry. Lines can be "cleaned up" by gently scraping the dry ink away with a toothpick.
2. Working in a well-ventilated area, use spray adhesive to adhere the cardstock to the frame backing. Reassemble the frame with the inked glass (inked side against the cardstock) and the cardstock-covered backing.
3. Paint the numbers dark brown; once completely dry, paint red. When the red paint is completely dry, lightly sand off the red paint to reveal the brown paint. Glue the numbers to the frame. ❄

# Paper Wreath

## SHOPPING LIST

- 20 wood spring-type clothespins
- old maps and colorful papers (lightweight scrapbook paper, pages from books, etc.)
- 16" square foam core board
- 10 25mm jingle bells (we used 5 red and 5 green)
- ½" wide twill tape
- craft glue
- hot glue gun
- craft knife

1. Use craft glue to adhere a cut-to-fit map paper strip to one side of each clothespin.

2. Cut a 14" diameter foam core board circle with an 8½" diameter center hole.

3. Beginning along one long edge, accordion pleat about sixty 5" x 8" pieces of assorted papers. Fold each paper in half; glue the inner fold together.

4. Evenly spacing the pins around the circle, hot glue the wood side of each clothespin to the circle, placing the clip toward the center. Hot glue the pleated papers between the pins.

5. Tie 5" lengths of twill tape to each bell. Clip the bells to every other clothespin on the wreath.

Finished size: 16½" diameter

# Christmas Countdown

## SHOPPING LIST

- 11¼" square papier-mache box with 25 drawers
- assorted scrapbook paper and cardstock
- old book with aged pages
- assorted charms, ribbons, buttons, plastic mirror hardware, knobs, snaps, and other decorative elements (some elements have numbers)
- rub-on numbers
- craft glue

1. Cut 1" strips of paper from the book and glue along the box sides and top.
2. Glue scrapbook paper or cardstock to each drawer. Attach the knobs to some drawers. Glue the other decorative elements to the drawers and add the numbers 1-25. Place a small gift or treat in each drawer.

# Paper Garlands

## SHOPPING LIST

- old book with aged pages
- map paper
- string and large eye needle
- 8mm red wood beads
- round metal-rimmed tags
- alphabet tags to spell "Make It"
- craft glue

For the fan and bead garland, begin along one long edge and accordion pleat 2" x 3" aged paper pieces. Fold the paper in half and glue into a fan shape. Thread the desired number of fans and beads on the desired length string.

For the tag garland, stack about 10 1" x 3½" aged paper pieces. Cut 2 long lengths of string. Using 1 end of each string, knot lengths together at the stack center. Cut fringe on the paper edges. Cut map paper circles slightly smaller than the metal-rimmed tags; glue the circles to the tags. Thread the desired number of metal-rimmed tags, alphabet tags, and beads on the strings, with the fringed paper as the divider between the words.

# Cards & Stationery Box

Glue patterned cardstock inside the lid of a vintage cigar box. Cut 8½" x 5½" cardstock pieces and fold in half. Personalize the cards with scrapbook paper, cardstock, small tags, rub-on letters, and charms. Place the cards in the box. ❄

Card finished size: 4¼" x 5½"

# Tags & Cards

## SHOPPING LIST

- assorted cardstock
- tracing paper
- ¼" hole punch
- assorted stickers and small tags
- assorted rubber stamps and ink
- glitter
- chipboard letters
- rub-on letters and motifs
- assorted ribbons
- thin jute twine
- brads
- craft glue

1. For tags, trace the pattern (page 16) to cut tags from the cardstock. Embellish the tags as desired. We stamped multiple phrases, sayings, and names, and added stickers, rub-ons, and chipboard letters. Thread ribbon or twine through holes punched at the tag tops.
2. For the cards, cut 3½" x 8" cardstock pieces and fold in half. Embellish the cards as desired. We added glitter accents, rub-on motifs, and cut 3" circles from coordinating cardstock and then attached them to the cards with brads. You can also decorate the circles with glitter and rub-on letters.

# Bookmark Paperclips

Super-size paperclips make great bookmarks! Pair each clip with vintage notions, such as buckles and buttons. Just layer a wool felt shape, the paperclip, and the notions. Add some wool yarn, cardstock, or an initial charm for extra interest and glue the components together. The standard-size paperclips below were made with felt, scrapbooking components, buttons, and a few bits of jewelry. The possibilities are endless! ❄

# Paint Chip Bookmarks

## SHOPPING LIST

- large paint chip samples from the paint store
- patterned scrapbook papers
- 1/4" dia. circle punch
- stickers and washi tapes
- 5/8"w twill tape
- craft glue

Decorate each paint chip sample as desired and trim to 2" x 6". Knot the twill tape through a hole punched near the top. ❄

# Glittery Noel

## SHOPPING LIST

- chipboard letters (N and L are 8" high)
- glittered cardstock
- acrylic paint to match cardstock
- small paintbrush
- cardboard scraps
- green felt scraps and red buttons
- craft glue
- tracing paper

1. Draw around each letter on the cardstock wrong side; be sure to draw the letters in reverse. Cut along the drawn lines. Paint the edges of each letter. Glue the cardstock to each letter.
2. Glue the letters together. Glue small strips of cardboard between the letters to hold the letters together.
3. Trace the holly patterns (page 16) onto tracing paper and cut out. Use the pattern to cut 2 holly leaves from felt. Glue the leaves and buttons to the letter N.

# Keepsake Shadow Box

## SHOPPING LIST

- 5" x 7" unfinished wood shadow box
- acrylic paint and paintbrush
- assorted scrapbook papers and cardstock
- patterned scrapbook paper with words (ours says "merry merry")
- 1/4" dia. circle punch
- craft glue
- disposable foam brush
- mica flakes
- vintage holiday keepsake
- rub-on letters
- thin red jute twine
- mini snowflake punch
- pom-pom trim

1. Paint the shadow box inside and out. Adhere cardstock or scrapbook paper to the box inside back. Cut simple trees from scrapbook paper and adhere to the background. Decorate a tree with punched "ornament" circles. Add a layered tag using words.
2. Use the foam brush to spread glue on the box bottom ledge. Glue the keepsake to the ledge. Sprinkle mica flakes on the glue around the keepsake.
3. For the mini banner, cut small cardstock pennants and use rub-on letters to spell "Christmas." Glue pennants to a length of red twine.
4. Reassemble the shadow box. Glue the mini banner, trim, and punched snowflakes to the shadow box.

# Cardholder

Show off holiday wishes to you and yours with this clever cardholder. Spray florist card picks silver and decorate by wrapping with beaded wire, ribbon bows, charms, and beaded dangles. Add foam and moss to a simple white vase, insert the picks, and tie on a ribbon bow. ❄

# Clothespins

With a few bits of scrapbook paper, some wooden clothespins, and glue, you can easily whip up bunches of these cute clothespins. Just glue cut-to-fit paper strips to the clothespin fronts—super simple! Use them to hang Christmas cards on a string, as gift bag closures, or add a mini magnet to the back to use on the fridge. ❄

# Holiday Vase

For a quick and elegant gift, glue glittery scrapbook paper around a 9"h cylindrical glass vase. Embellish with a scalloped paper border and two lengths of 1/4"w ribbon threaded through a large 4-hole button. Use floss to tie layered preprinted tags to the button.

Fill the vase with fresh or faux greenery.

# Packages

Wrap your gifts in the classified ads from the daily paper. Add a paper band (or two), ribbon, and rub-ons. Or place a special gift in a natural wood box, top with cardstock, string, and a personalized tag. Newspaper or vintage paper accordion-pleated circles, tied paper tassels, or even a photocopy of a treasured family photo replace the standard ribbon bow.

# Patterns

Production Team: Technical Writer – Mary Sullivan Hutcheson; Technical Associate – Lisa Lancaster; Editorial Writer – Susan Frantz Wiles; Senior Graphic Artist – Lora Puls; Graphic Artist – Leia Morshedi.